TOP TIPS:
RUNNING HOLIDAY CLUBS

Vicki Brackpool, Helen Franklin and Steve Hutchinson

Copyright © Scripture Union 2010
First published 2010
ISBN 978 184427 541 0

Scripture Union England and Wales
207–209 Queensway, Bletchley,
Milton Keynes, MK2 2EB, England
Email: info@scriptureunion.org.uk
Website: www.scriptureunion.org.uk

Scripture Union Australia
Locked Bag 2, Central Coast Business
Centre, NSW 2252
Website: www.scriptureunion.org.au

Scripture Union USA
PO Box 987, Valley Forge, PA 19482
Website: www.scriptureunion.org

Scriptures and additional materials
quoted are from the *Good News Bible*
© 1994 published by the Bible
Societies/HarperCollins Publishers Ltd
UK, *Good News Bible* © American
Bible Society 1966, 1971, 1976,
1992. Used with permission.

The right of Vicki Brackpool, Helen
Franklin and Steve Hutchinson to be
identified as authors of this work has
been asserted by them in accordance
with the Copyright, Designs and
Patents Act 1988.

British Library Cataloguing-in-
Publication Data: a catalogue record
of this book is available from the
British Library.

Printed and bound in Singapore by
Tien Wah Press Ltd

Logo, cover design, internal design:
www.splash-design.co.uk

Internal illustrations: Colin Smithson

Typesetting: Richard Jefferson, Author
and Publisher Services

Scripture Union is an
international Christian charity working
with churches in more than 130
countries, providing resources to bring
the good news about Jesus Christ to
children, young people and families
and to encourage them to develop
spiritually through the Bible and
prayer.

As well as our network of volunteers,
staff and associates who run holidays,
church-based events and school
Christian groups, we produce a wide
range of publications and support
those who use our resources through
training programmes.

CONTENTS

INTRODUCTION

Holiday clubs can take a huge variety of forms. In this book we are talking about a Bible-based event, usually running over several days and possibly up to a whole week, including the weekends at both ends.

Holiday clubs are usually aimed at children between the ages of 4 and 11 (primary school age), but may include activities for under-5s or 11 to 14s. The team running the event may include junior team members aged 14 to 18 or even 12 to 18.

Holiday clubs are often run as an outreach to the community by a church. They may include special events for the whole family, and often conclude with an all-age service.

The Top Tips given in this book relate to holiday clubs that follow a biblical theme, perhaps the life story of a Bible character or various aspects of Jesus' ministry, with the aim of helping children respond in some appropriate way to the message of the Bible.

Holiday clubs generally include some activities all together, perhaps singing, prayers, Bible stories, drama, memory verses, quizzes or aerobics, and some activities in small groups, such as reading the Bible, chatting about questions, crafts, games and prayers.

PART ONE – BIBLE FOUNDATIONS

There are no recorded instances of holiday clubs being run in the Bible! However, there *is* plenty about teaching children God's commands and making disciples of all people, and quite a few instances where we can assume that the whole family was involved, such as Jesus going to Jerusalem with his family and the people listening to the Bible in Nehemiah's day (Nehemiah 8). Let's take a look at some of those and see how they help us think about running better holiday clubs.

Welcoming children

In New Testament times children were considered of little importance, yet in the following two passages we see how important they are to Jesus. Holiday clubs are usually for children, so these verses encourage us to do our best for them, in order to bring them to Jesus.

> **In reality…**
> To help children feel welcome at our holiday club, we make the venue look really great; we are sure it is a safe and comfortable place for children and we do our best to be ready on time to welcome the children so they feel at home straight away.

… in Jesus' name

And whoever welcomes in my name one such child as this, welcomes me' (Matthew 18:5). Imagine the scene, with the disciples discussing who is the greatest in the kingdom of heaven. They look around at each other – could it be Peter, the preacher through whom 3,000 would be converted at Pentecost, or John who would sit next to Jesus at the Last Supper, or James the other one of the inner three? Now look to Jesus, who has called a child. Jesus is saying some amazing things about the kingdom, but he is also surely raising the status of the child: 'Here, adults, look at this child.'

Jesus blessed the children

'Some people brought children to Jesus for him to place his hands on them, but the disciples scolded the people. When Jesus noticed this, he was angry and said to his disciples, "Let the children come to me, and do not stop them, because the Kingdom of God belongs to such as these. I assure you that whoever does not receive the Kingdom of God like a child will never enter it." Then he took the children in his arms, placed his hands on each of them, and blessed them' (Mark 10:13–16).

Jesus was angry with his disciples for trying to stop the parents bringing children to him. No doubt they thought they were doing what Jesus wanted, but they didn't know how highly Jesus valued children. He invited the children to come to him, then placed his hands on them and blessed them.

We show how we value children by the standards that we aim for in our holiday club, and by the amount of time and effort we put in. By doing the best we can, and giving the children a great time, we show that we care for them as Jesus does.

Our role as adults

The great commission

Jesus' last words to his disciples commanded them to: 'Go, then, to all peoples everywhere and make them my disciples: baptize them in the name of the Father, the Son, and the Holy Spirit, and teach them to obey everything I have commanded you. And I will be with you always, to the end of the age' (Matthew 28:19,20).

Running a holiday club is part of the way we fulfil this command from Jesus. We are going to the children around us. Our aim is to make them disciples. We are not just trying to get them to come to the holiday club, or even to church every Sunday, but to teach them to obey Jesus and become his disciples.

Moses' instructions

When Moses reminded the people of God's laws he told them: 'Love the LORD your God with all your heart, with all your soul, and with all your strength. Never forget these commands that I am giving you today. Teach them to your children' (Deuteronomy 6:5–7).

As part of God's people today, we are instructed to teach God's commands to children. Our holiday club needs to include this, and not just in what we say from the front. We repeat God's commandments as we live them out – 'actions speak louder than words' is never truer than when working with children.

Eli and Samuel

In 1 Samuel 3 God spoke to the child Samuel after the adults, who should have obeyed God, ignored him. It's a great story showing how God calls people of all ages who are willing to listen and obey, and uses them to spread his message. Like Eli, we often don't expect God to speak

Think about…
What might God want to say to us through the children at our holiday club? Or do we assume that God only speaks through us adults?

to children! As the story of Samuel illustrates, God does call children and equips them to serve him. We can be confident that children *are* able to hear and respond to God.

Other passages

There are many other Bible passages relevant to working with children. In particular, you and your team may wish to look at Psalm 78:1–7 and Acts 17:22–31.

Communicating the Bible

Jesus taught the people with stories

Jesus spoke about the kingdom of God to his listeners using stories of familiar activities, such as that of the sower that we find in Matthew 13:1–23. He grabbed their attention with his stories, which contain eternal truths. Interestingly, he hardly ever explained the meaning of his stories and, even when he did, it was only to his close friends. Stories are a great way for us to communicate the truths of the Bible to children. We can provoke their interest and help them to think about God and the Bible using stories as a way in.

Timothy, remember…

Paul wrote to Timothy, '… you remember that ever since you were a child, you have known the Holy Scriptures, which are able to give you the wisdom that leads to salvation through faith in Christ Jesus' (2 Timothy 3:15).

Those of us who were taught the Bible as children have a wonderful advantage, as we have known this wisdom since then. Why is this wisdom so good? Because it leads to salvation. How does this salvation work? Through faith. Through faith in whom? Faith in Christ Jesus. What a great summary of what a knowledge of the Bible can do for us. This is why the Bible is right at the centre of Scripture Union holiday club programmes. That way we can have an impact for life on the children with whom we work.

> **Think about…**
> How will we help the children get to know the Bible in such a way that they gain the wisdom that Paul speaks about in 2 Timothy 3:15, and so find faith in Jesus?

2

PART TWO – IN THEORY

What is a holiday club?

St Andrew's run theirs for a week in August for 5 to 11-year-olds using the latest Scripture Union programme; Main Street Church's is once a week through the summer holidays, for any child accompanied by an adult, offering play and craft activities linked to a Bible story; The Chapel on the Green hold theirs for three days at February half term for school years 3 to 6, focusing on sport and creative arts. And they are all called holiday clubs!

Christ Church Selly Park has run a week-long holiday club for several years. They follow it up with a 'Christmas craft' afternoon culminating in a Christingle service. Last summer they opened the church one weekday each week through the school holidays for parents and children to 'drop in', and at Easter they will run a two-day club.

Think about...
What do you want your holiday club to do? The answer to this will help you to decide what to run where and when, and which children to target.

As you can see, holiday clubs can take various shapes and forms, and run for a varied length of time. Some include Christian teaching while others will simply be activity-based. For the purposes of this book we are concentrating on clubs that include Bible teaching, as there are extra considerations for these.

Who is it for?

You may be able to include all of the following in your club, or decide to focus on a particular group:

*   *Churched children* – children who attend church.

- *Unchurched children* – either friends of churched children, or drawn by publicity or personal contact.
- *Limited age range*. Many clubs run for children aged 5–11, but some find this puts off the eldest, who think it is too young for them. If you particularly want to target this age group you might need to limit the age range to Key Stage 2 children (8–11s).
- *Families*. You might run the whole week as a family club (although there can be some major issues because of young children, and limited places available) or simply invite them to some special events.

Think about...

If the club is mainly for churched children, how will it differ from your regular work on Sundays? What special considerations will you need to make if inviting unchurched children to the club? What events would be appropriate for families?

What will be the hallmarks?

- *Fun!* This is a holiday activity and you will want children to enjoy it.
- *Relationships*: good and appropriate friendships growing between children and leaders, and with families.
- *Lots of involvement*: activities and input that are relevant to the children and to their world, and which help them see where the Bible and the Christian faith have meaning for them.

- *Pace but not speed*. Children should not be watching the clock wondering when it will end, so aim for a sense of anticipation of what comes next but with time to complete craft activities etc.

What do I need to think about before I begin?

Key questions to answer before you start planning:
- *Who*? Look back at the section 'Who is it for?' Who will form your team?
- *Why*? This will affect the choice of material used.
- *What*? Will you use published material or create your own? Your decision will be guided by the answers to the two questions above.
- *When*? Choose dates to suit both children and team members. Find out if there are other clubs running in the area and aim to avoid clashes of dates – or consider working together. Don't always assume that summer is best; half term, when less is happening, may be better. Consider too when fits best with the church's calendar.
- *How long*? Think carefully about the number of days and length of sessions. This may be guided by age of children and availability of team members.
- *Where*? Is church the best venue, or would a neutral place, such as a school or community centre, be more suitable? Could it even be run in the open air? Consider the adequacy of facilities, any restrictions on numbers placed by fire regulations, etc.

Consider these areas too:
Links to children's families How will you build contact? Could you run any family activities as part of the club? Who else in the church might help with these?

Links to church Where does it fit in to your plans for children's work, and with the church's ongoing evangelism and discipleship programme? How might you build on this to draw children further into church life (not just through Sunday worship!)?

Links into the community What opportunities will the club offer for your church to be more involved with the local community?

Legal requirements Children's safety is paramount when running a club and you will need to show that you have taken the appropriate action. Check the Ofsted regulations to ensure you comply with current legislation, and that you meet your church's requirements regarding safeguarding children (child protection). There is some useful information in the holiday club section of the Scripture Union website.

> ### In reality…
> Mary found that the best way to recruit team members for the club was to talk about it during a service, but then to ask people directly, often for specific roles.

Team How many team members will you need to run an effective, safe club? Aim for a balance of gender and age, if possible, and a mix of people experienced in children's work alongside those new to it but willing to try. Offer everyone training and recruit sufficient team members in advance. Aim for a mix of people who can cover different areas of the work: leading small groups, administration, crafts, games, music, teaching the Bible in words and ways children can understand, refreshments, first aid, etc. No one person can do everything, and the overall leader will need to delegate tasks appropriately. Training your team will help new people to develop the necessary skills, but will also refresh those who are experienced and allow you to be clear about the club's aims, the style of work (how you will handle different children, any issues, etc.) and talk through specific Bible teaching.

Faith development

In reality…

Joe, aged 9, will come to the club because his friends Isaac and Oliver want to be there, and he wants to be where they are. His faith is affected positively by that of his friends.

Tom, aged 11, isn't sure that he believes in God: he'd like to, but he's not going to do so just because his parents do. He's not rebelling but sorting things in his mind before he decides about faith in God.

Just as children go through stages of physical development, so their faith may develop too.

When you see 6-year-old Hannah at the shops, you smile and say, 'Hello, Hannah!' So when at church you say that God loves her, she believes you, because you, his follower, show love to her. She's at the stage of experience shaping her faith.

We can't generalise and say that all children of these ages are at a particular stage of faith, but it's helpful to stop and consider whether you are teaching the Bible and working in ways that are appropriate for where their sense of faith might be. For more on this topic see *Top Tips on Encouraging Faith to Grow* or *Children Finding Faith*, both published by Scripture Union.

In reality…
With lots of older boys at their holiday club, the team at St Andrew's had 'Coach's bench' in one corner of the room, where children could sit individually with a leader to ask their own questions about God.

Learning styles

Not every child learns things in the same way: some take in most through listening, some learn best if the information comes visually, while others learn through doing.

You can read more about learning styles in *Top Tips on Inspiring all Kinds of Learners*, but keep it in mind as you plan your holiday club so that you include activities that cover the range of learning styles. If you know a school teacher, ask their advice about ways to vary the style of activities.

Working with unchurched children

If bringing more children into contact with the church is a key aim for your club, then this is really important! But also keep it in mind for those who might attend with churched friends. A few simple steps will help a lot.

- Make no assumptions about what they will know, so explain the background to Bible passages as appropriate.
- Avoid jargon. Use ordinary words and ideas that any child can understand. See *Top Tips on Explaining the Cross* for some help with this.

- If you include a quiz, make sure there are general knowledge questions at which a child with no Bible knowledge can shine.
- Choosing materials. Look again at your aims before deciding what to use. Select something that will work well for the children you are targeting and the team leading the club.

What happens after it?

Any club will be more effective if it is part of an ongoing programme. Aim for year-round contact with the children through one or more of the following: activity days, midweek club, family activities, a school Christian club, inviting children and families to special church services. Be aware that this last one can be a huge step for some, so prepare the church to be welcoming and plan service outlines that are user-friendly for those not used to church. There is a useful 'Year round ministry options' document on the Scripture Union website.

In reality...
One church asked their mission committee to organise family events every 6 to 8 weeks through the year following the holiday club regularly – bonfire, Christmas party, pancake party, etc. At each event tickets were available for the next one, so that even unchurched families got into the habit of coming to a special event.

PART THREE – PRACTICAL IDEAS

3

This section will provide you with basic information about the practicalities of running a club. It will help you to feel confident as you begin to schedule meetings and put things into place for your fantastic Bible-based holiday club!

Useful websites and helpful publications are listed in the *Resources* section on page 32 of this book. Further information is also available on the Scripture Union holiday club bulletin board on the SU website.

Planning (time and schedule)

Prayer

One of the keys to good planning is communication. Begin by meeting to bring your ideas before God – communication with him throughout is essential! Often this is forgotten or left until the end of a meeting and rushed. Prayer should be a priority and is a great opportunity to gather people together and share initial thoughts, engaging people as part of a team right at the outset. You may invite the whole church or perhaps ask them to continue to pray as you meet with a smaller team. The church can be involved through prayer even if they are not able to be part of the event. Consider:

- The event is about reaching children and families.
- Children could produce bookmarks to prompt prayer.
- Housebound people can pray!
- Encourage prayer triplets.

Prayer is important in all that we do, and being sure of God's will in taking things forward is fundamental.

Think about...
Providing children at church with a small card that says, 'I am praying for my friend _ _ _ _ _ to come to holiday club.'

Meetings

Gathering together is important for building team morale, gelling together and enabling everyone to feel a part of what is happening.

Here is a sample plan of meetings:

First meeting (12 months before):
Get together to share ideas and input. Decide whether or not the club should go ahead, and agree dates and venue as soon as you can.

Second meeting (9–3 months before):
Begin planning the programme, including: Bible topics and themes; team roles; craft ideas; music; resources.

Final briefing (6 weeks before):
Recap to date. Go through the daily programme and train your team, finalise plans and pray again!

In reality…

A holiday club leader uses PowerPoint in meetings. The team are then able to follow on screen and know what stage they are at. He types notes directly into the PowerPoint so everyone can see and correct where necessary. This saves time checking notes and means less paper!

This is an idea of what you might do. As a leader you may decide that you need to meet more as things progress.

When inviting people to meetings be clear about how long you will be – one and a half to two hours is about right. Think about what will be covered before the meeting, gather helpful resources and try to stick to your timings. Begin by outlining what is going to be discussed and ensure you encourage involvement. Taking notes for records is very helpful! Think about your meeting venue. A church hall sometimes isn't the best option if it is cold and damp. Refreshments and snacks often go down well too!

Venue

One of the first things a child notices is what they see immediately before them. How will they feel when they step into your chosen venue? What can you do to make the environment welcoming and exciting for a child? Perhaps you might use colourful bunting, flags, pictures, posters, rugs and cushions. Most venues have room for adding things to the wall or hanging things up. Make sure you are aware of fire regulations and check the insurance policy.

Think about…
How will the way you decorate the venue enhance the club's theme? Are there items you can make, borrow or buy which will highlight the theme and create an imaginative display for the children? Will you need extra signs up or footprints on the ground to follow to the entrance?

Publicity

This is the first point of contact and should be accurate and well produced. Things to include: holiday club theme; that it's Bible based; venue; dates; times; need to register; contact info for further enquiries.

When creating publicity make it:

- inviting
- colourful
- easy to read
- not too much text

- something that chidlren and adults will access.

Visiting local schools to do an assembly closer to the event is often a good way to capture imagination, perhaps by demonstrating some of the programme. Whatever you do, publicity is key to making people aware of your great club!

There is information on CPO, a printing company, in the back of all SU holiday club material. They can supply a wide range of resources, such as posters, T-shirts and invitations, themed for a specific club.

Enabling others (the team)

Working with a team

Teams can be great to work in, and sometimes challenging. Things to consider when working with a team are: time, commitment, availability, experience, young leaders (under-18s), legal requirements (including CRB checks). See the *Resources* page for where to find more information.

You will need to know availability and an idea of what experience each team member has. It may be useful to ask about gifts and interests in order to make the best use of skills and talents as you try to match team members with the available roles. Some will be great at speaking to parents as they arrive at the event; others may prefer running the technology for you, or making the squash.

Young leaders are often fantastic and thrive on being part of something like this. Use their skills, and encourage them with responsibility where appropriate.

Training a team

The time you spend on training will depend on your team and availability. This may be worked into the final briefing. It is an opportunity to:

- discuss the programme outline
- do some teambuilding exercises
- answer questions
- address concerns about lack of skills
- talk about setting boundaries
- decide how to handle problems.

Some team members will want to know what is expected of them. Others won't mind not knowing. Try to provide a comfortable place where people will feel at ease. Scripture Union always produces a training piece on each holiday club DVD – a great asset to training!

In reality…

One holiday club leader organised two team members to provide breakfast each morning for the whole team. While eating breakfast together, the team looked at the passage for the day, discussed the main teaching emphasis and had an opportunity to ask questions themselves. This was relaxed and gave clarity, giving the team a bit more confidence with the task.

Finance

Drawing up a financial summary of costs at the outset will put you in a good position. It will give you an idea of what the club will cost to run and mean that you have a figure to work towards. How will you pay for it? Can the church afford it? Will you need to fundraise? Will you charge a small fee for children to attend? These are all important questions to ask. You may like to nominate one member of your team to be in charge of finances.

Think about...
What will you need to buy? Will you give prizes away? How will you manage a budget?

Once you have a ballpark figure to work with you can consider ideas for funding, for example: coffee mornings; encouraging everyone in church to give; asking people to donate specific prizes; a fundraiser linked with the theme of the club – a fish and chip supper for the last Sunday service sponsored by the local fish and chip shop for *Rocky's Plaice* (SU holiday club) in return for some advertising on posters?

Often people want to buy things to help with a holiday club. Collect receipts and ask them to put money in the offering so that the church and holiday club leaders know at the end what the event has cost. Churches need to be aware of the reality in order to budget for next time!

During the event

Team
Ensure enough time has been allocated prior to children and parents arriving for communication with the team, to pray, answer queries, look

at the programme and recap who's doing what. This time can easily go so perhaps providing breakfast for team members to encourage teambuilding might entice them to arrive earlier! Remember, you will also need to plan time for setting up.

Ending the day with a team briefing to get an idea of how the team are getting on with things and how the children seemed to cope is a good idea!

Welcome!

There will be a whole host of different feelings for children and parents as they make their way to an event for the first time, especially if they've not met you before. On arrival it is important that the first team members a parent and child come into contact with are welcoming to both! You may have someone in your team whom parents and children will know well who is involved in the local school or runs a toddler group in the area.

Think carefully about who takes on the welcoming role as there are likely to be queries that need answering, registration forms to deal with, collection tickets to hand out and groups to organise. If you have decided to ask parents to pre-register their children this will save time on the first day. From experience, it is very useful to have a team leader close by at registration on day one or at least someone who has experienced this kind of responsibility before. Young leaders can be paired with other team members to pick up these kinds of skills, and vice versa.

> **Think about...**
> How will you register the children for your event? Will you ask for registration details beforehand? If yes, how will you collect the registration details? If you decide to do registration on day one, then be prepared!

Parents

Some parents will be very nervous of leaving their children and others will not be fazed at all. Listen to them and deal with any of their concerns appropriately. Ensure your team are aware of how to deal with any difficulties that may occur.

Have an alphabetical list of parents' emergency contact details easily accessible at all times.

The presentation

Programme

You will need to think about what kind of structure you will have within a session at your event. The most common structure follows this pattern: group work; up-front time; group work; up-front time. It is good to start with group time while children arrive, and good to finish in a group in order for a group leader to safely dismiss children with the right parent. There are many aspects to consider within your programme, such as, will the children arrive and go straight to their group? This can lend itself well to providing a task which all can be involved in no matter what time they arrive. Other things to think about include quizzes, games, how to incorporate the theme, memory verse(s), drama, daily challenge, rewards system, etc. Here is a sample daily programme based on running for 2 hrs 15 mins which you can adjust:

- *Welcome and settle* (10 mins) – welcome children into groups, begin task.
- *Up front 1* (35 mins) – warm up (aerobics), challenge (such as against the clock, move as many chocolate beans from the cup to the bowl as you can using a straw and your mouth), song, story or talk, prayer.

- *Group time* (50 mins) – drinks, Bible engagement (a closer look at the day's passage), prayer, games, crafts.
- *Up front 2* (35 mins) – recap day's story, quiz, drama, memory verse, creative prayer.

In reality…

One club included some very random things in their programme just for fun! 'Word of the day' was delivered creatively by a team member popping their head through a curtain and saying the word. The challenge the next day was to remember the interesting word, which sometimes related to the teaching. The children really grew to like 'Stan the word man' and learned some new words too!

Shape this to work for you in light of your aims and the gifts within your team. This is a guide to help you think about timings and content. Remember that, on top of this, you will need preparation time before and time afterwards to clear up and prepare for the next day.

Having a consistent programme where possible will enable the children to be aware of what is coming next and to look forward to aspects of it.

Think about…

Will you include a reward system at your event? Discuss this as a team and decide together how you will tackle this. Ensure it is inclusive and give everyone a chance to participate.

Delivery

Discuss how you will deliver the holiday club, and who will deliver which part. Often a programme has one leader who keeps an eye on timing and may lead some sessions from the front; they may also have a co-leader for up-front sessions. Communication is important! It's easy to get caught up in the action once things are running, so take some time to think beforehand about the tone of your voice when you are talking to the children. Vary your pace and be careful to speak clearly. You need to keep the children interested and capture their imaginations. Being aware of how you come across is important. You might use visuals, music or drama.

The team should all know their roles and understand what they need to do. The programme leader may have to step in if a team member has popped off to do something and forgotten they're up next. Essentially, this is a key role and an important part of keeping things running smoothly as you move from one thing to the next.

Problems

Hopefully there won't be many of these! However, it is a good idea to allocate someone as a 'floater', ie not tied to any one activity, who can pick up problems and deal with them calmly, effectively and quickly. This could be done on a rotation basis so that it isn't down to one team member every day. Check registration forms beforehand for issues specific to individual children that may cause problems.

Technology

Technology doesn't just mean using a computer or laptop! There are always pros and cons of using technology so have back-up if you can. PowerPoint can work well for telling children (and team members!) what is coming next in the programme and providing song words. The same slides can be used each day and need not hold lots of information; a striking picture and large text is enough.

Video is another aspect that can work very well (check whether or not you need a licence to show your chosen film clips). A video quiz is often a popular item where children are shown a 3–5-minute clip and then asked questions based on observation. This could be for points or just for fun! Every Scripture Union holiday club includes a DVD as part of the programme.

Consider using your younger leaders to organise and operate

your equipment; they are often great with technology.

Technology shouldn't replace interaction with children but enhance it. A balance is needed. For those without access to these resources, don't panic! A good holiday club doesn't require a laptop – although it helps, it's not a necessity. An OHP can be used as a prompt, too, and works well for song words, memory verses, etc.

Music

Using music to create an atmosphere works well and you could have different tracks when the children are doing different activities. Sometimes a short sound clip as an introduction to part of your programme is a great indication of what's coming next, and the children will begin to recognise it.

Part of your programme will be about engaging children in worship. You may be blessed with a number of gifted musicians in your team which is great. If you have someone willing to take a lead in sorting out the music that's brilliant. Don't worry if you've not got musicians; CDs can work well, backing tracks or other tracks to sing along to. There are alternative ways of providing music without musicians.

This is another role that can be delegated.

Think about…

What volume of music will work best for your venue? Will you need microphones? Who will organise that? Will you need other equipment for the band if there is one?

Resources

You would be surprised to find that between the local churches in your area there are probably lots of materials sitting in cupboards! Go and find them! Perhaps asking a church about holiday club resources will open up conversations on working together. Sharing and pooling resources with other churches is a great way of saving cost, and if they've run a particular club previously they may have all sorts of other things to provide you with, too.

There are a great number of Scripture Union resources listed on page 32 and on the inside covers, which should bring you more inspiration! You can also contact SU or visit the SU website to find out about available materials. Getting in touch with your local SU worker to talk about ideas and access other resources could also be a great way to open up other channels of working.

After the event

Holiday clubs are fantastic events for sharing Jesus with children, but it doesn't have to stop there! Once you've cleared up, shared together, thanked God and taken in all that you have achieved, set aside some time to discuss what steps you might take to build the contact with the children and families in the community.

Think about…

Be careful when you think about how to stay in touch with children. Facebook and other social networking sites are not the best choice. They can easily be mistreated and encourage hidden communication. Communication should be kept to a minimum for the protection of all. Consider child protection and safety issues and make sure you brief your team appropriately.

You might consider:

- a postcard to each child to thank them for coming – this is a safe way of communicating
- a follow-up assembly a few weeks later
- a holiday club reunion of some sort – an event which involves the family (such as a family picnic or a family praise party, or an all-day holiday club reunion where parents and carers are invited to join in the barbecue at tea time).

You can find more ideas on the holiday clubs pages at www.scriptureunion.org.uk, or contact your local SU worker to talk it through.

Whatever you decide to do, follow up is key in continuing the work that God has begun at your holiday club!

TEN TOP TIPS

- Pray together. Ask God what he wants you to share from the Bible and with whom. This will bring a correct focus from the start.

- Plan well in advance. Do your best to stick to deadlines!

- Communicate. Ensure that you share, plan and reflect together.

- Publicise in good time. Don't rush this.

- Build a good team. Plan together, invite people to take on specific roles and be clear about them.

- Involve the church. Ask the church to be involved before, during and after the event.

- Watch the children. Are they enjoying it? Are they joining in?

- Double check everything for safety. Consider team issues, allergies, venue, crafts, electrics, fire, child protection, insurance, ISA/CRB.

- Keep it simple and flexible. Flexibility is not a failure, it's a strength!

- Enjoy yourselves! Talk to the children and the team members about what they are enjoying too.

RESOURCES

Websites

www.scriptureunion.org.uk/HolidayandMidweekClubs/2368.id – Scripture Union's holiday club website; the 'Downloads' section includes information on the legal requirements for running a club.
www.ofsted.gov.uk – official government guidance; for information on whether or not you need to register your holiday club type 'registration not required' into the 'Search' box.

Scripture Union holiday club material

Mission:Rescue – stories of God rescuing his people, from Exodus 1–15, with a spies/secret agents theme
Rocky's Plaice – stories of Peter from Acts, set in a fish and chip shop
Showstoppers! – God's great plan for salvation using five stories from Old and New Testaments

For more titles see inside back cover and the holiday club website.

Other publications

Top Tips on Encouraging Faith to Grow
Top Tips on Inspiring all Kinds of Learners
Top Tips on Explaining the Cross

Francis Bridger, *Children Finding Faith – Exploring a child's response to God*, Scripture Union, 2003

SU booklets to use with children who have heard the good news of Jesus and want to respond:
Friends with Jesus (for 5–8s)
Me + Jesus (for 8–9s)
Jesus = friendship for ever (for 10–12s)